CARVING JACK-O'-LANTERNS

HAYNER PUBLIC LIBRARY DISTRICT
ALTON, ILLINOIS

OVERDUES .10 PER DAY MAXIMUM FINE
COST OF BOOKS. LOST OR DAMAGED
BOOKS ADDITIONAL $5.00 SERVICE CHARGE.

HAYNER PLD/YOUTH

CARVING JACK-O'-LANTERNS

Sam Gendusa
SG
PRODUCTIONS
DAYTON, OREGON 97114

Copyright © 1988 Sam Gendusa.
All rights reserved. No part of this book may be reproduced or transmitted in any form or by any means, electronic or mechanical, recording or by any information storage and retrieval system, or photocopied, without permission in writing from the publisher.
S/G Productions, P.O. Box 432, Dayton, Oregon 97114

Library of Congress #88-92605
ISBN 0-9621071-0-7

Text edited by Arnold Ruse, Wordsmith Editing Service, Salem, Oregon.
Printing by Image Graphics & Litho, Inc., Portland, Oregon.
Typesetting by Irish Setter, Portland, Oregon.

Library of Congress Cataloging in Publication Data
Gendusa, Sam
Carving Jack-o'-Lanterns.
Summary: Discusses the history of carving jack-o'-lanterns, and gives technical information on how to carve, demonstrate and grow giant pumpkins.

NOTE ON CHAPTER NUMBERS:

The Celtic-inspired numbers that head each chapter chronicle the story of Halloween through imagery.

035.62
GEN
b14346939

CONTENTS

Introduction

A jack-o'-lantern is an event. I first became aware of that fact about twenty years ago when I first began carving giant pumpkins for exhibit in various schools. Small children seeing their first giant jack-o'-lanterns squealed with delight, as though the golden vegetables had suddenly, magically sprung to life. I saw their excitement reflected in the eyes of the larger "children"—their parents and teachers—who asked excitedly if these wondrous objects could be preserved for display the next year.

To the latter I responded as I've responded to audiences ever since: The jack-o'-lantern is a celebration of its season, and like any meaningful celebration, it should be fresh, spontaneous. It's not the object that matters so much, I explain; it's the affinity between the object and beholder that's important.

I must confess there have been times over the years when I've questioned both my sanity and my artistic integrity. Isn't there something a bit absurd, after all, about a grown man carving a silly face on an overgrown vegetable? But what is it about a jack-o'-lantern that triggers excited responses from young and old alike? How could I account for that glimmer of amused recognition that I saw year after year in the eyes of my audiences at shopping centers and pumpkin festivals? Had I tapped a primordial funny bone, or did it go deeper than that?

Keep in mind that I asked these questions from an artist's perspective. I was and am a sculptor, one who happens to have stumbled upon a unique folk art that appears to have its origins in prehistory but rises with renewed vigor every October 31.

As I researched the history of the lantern/mask and probed the mystique of the myths, legends and folklore of which it is so much a part, I became even more determined to explain and perpetuate pumpkin carving as an art form. This small book does not pretend to be a definitive history of the jack-o'-lantern, nor is it the last word on pumpkin carving and growing techniques. It is an artist's effort to share with you some of his inspiration, to spark your own curiosity and imagination. Happy carving!

Sam Gendusa

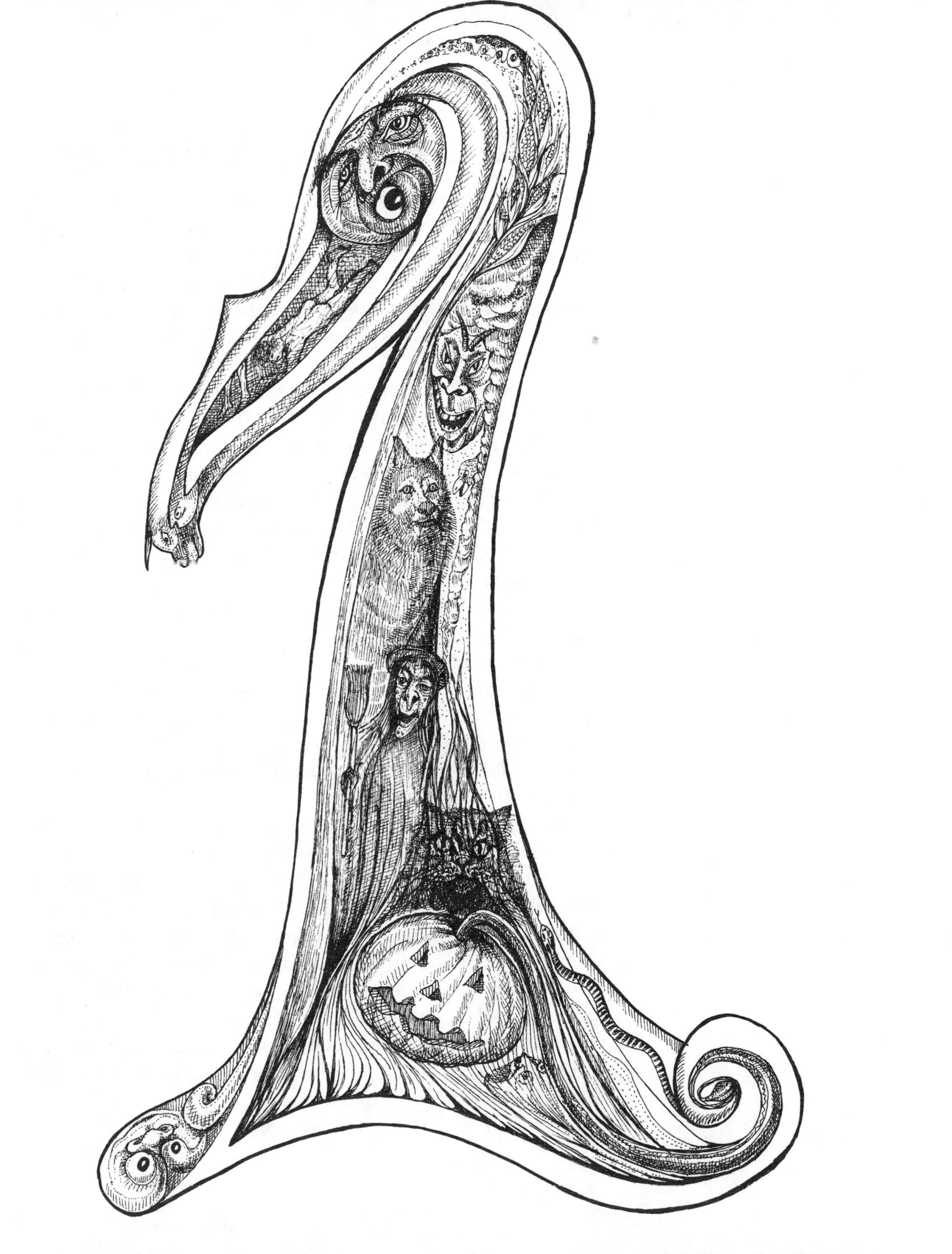

CHAPTER ONE • HISTORY

Chapter One: A History

Jack, so the story goes, could not enter Heaven, because he was a miser. Nor could he enter Hell, because he had played jokes on the Devil. As a result, Jack had to walk the earth with his lantern until Judgment Day. This charming Irish legend explains the name but not the meaning of one of the most curious and least understood symbols of the celebration of Halloween.

The updated version of the jack-o'-lantern illustrated on the cover of this book features a giant, 300-pound pumpkin with fog spewing from its mouth and nostrils—a modern-day gargoyle. The colored lights, placed both inside and outside the carving, illuminate the fog and create an image of fantasy and humor, which is what modern Halloween is all about. But it was not always that way. Let's try to imagine how it might have been.

The year is 2000 B.C., the place a settlement in Britain. A people called the Celts have established their influence over most of northern Europe and are successful farmers, traders and warriors. Their "calendar" is a circle of massive stones—we now call it Stonehenge—which not only permits them to determine the seasons, but also pinpoints special days for celebration and serves as a place for worship and ritual.

The Celts had been nomadic hunters and gatherers. The focus of their social life had been the campfire, around which they gathered to share tales of the hunt, communicate their ideas and feelings, and develop their cultural identity.

As they settled and turned to tilling crops, the campfire gave way to the bonfire, the occasional harvest became the annual harvest, a special time for communal rejoicing and sacrifice, and Stonehenge became the site of their ritualistic celebration, an extension of the pre-agrarian supper around the campfire. Millenia later, the great Gothic cathedrals would perform the same function.

The Celts celebrated New Year's Eve on what is now October 31, a date more clearly marking the "end" of the year to an agrarian society than our own December 31. The gods, they believed, must be thanked for the harvest and appeased as well, for the long darkness and decay of winter lay ahead. One god in particular, Samhain, lord of death, must receive his due. Samhain, the Celts believed, permitted the souls of the dead to return to earth on October 31 and evil spirits were afoot. It was a night of witches and devil worship. Only sacrifice to the sacred flame, and the incantations of their priests and teachers, the Druids, could protect the innocent.

The only fire permitted in the village that night of "The Rite of Change" was the bonfire at Stonehenge kindled by the branches from an oak tree, also held to be sacred, and fed by the sacrifices from the villagers' harvest. The people, dressed in animal skins to imitate a nature they could not fully understand, danced around the fire offering a portion of their crops to it and holding aloft unlighted lantern/masks, huge turnips carved into grotesque images to ward off the evil spirits.

Having made their sacrifices, the participants then mounted their lantern/masks, which had been filled with tallow or fat, on sticks and received from the priests flame from the sacred bonfire. They then returned to their homes to relight their hearth fires with the "light of their culture" made sacred by their sacrifices to the communal bonfire and the incantations of the Druids.

Vestiges of this powerfully symbolic ancient ritual are reflected in our own society: candlelight vigils, bonfire celebrations, costumes—and jack-o'-lanterns.

Another aspect to be considered as we look to the origins of the lantern/mask has its roots in battle. Ancient warriors, the Celts among them, severed the heads of vanquished foes, mounted them on poles, and displayed them in their ceremonies as not only trophies of victory, but as charms against the forces of evil. The practice would evolve to using carved heads to decorate dwellings, gateposts, door knockers, walking sticks, even furniture.

RITUAL OF THE LANTERN/MASKS

This reconstruction of the event which took place 4,000 years ago shows the Druid priest dressed in an animal skin taking a sample of fire from the sacred communal bonfire and lighting a lantern/mask. This celebration took place at summer's end, which was the Celtic New Year's Eve celebration.

They were celebrating the "rite of change" reflected in the wearing of animal skins, like the person wearing the set of antlers in the foreground. This festival took place in special places set aside for worship and sacrifice, one of them we now call Stonehenge.

Stonehenge is a prehistoric monument, originally constructed of wood 5,000 years ago; it was changed into stone 1,000 years later, and completed with an inner layer of stones 3,500 years ago.

Celtic scholars do not agree as to whether the Celtic people constructed Stonehenge or any of the other stone megaliths scattered throughout Britain and France. However, the Celtic people did use them, and these people (proto-Celtic people) constructed them as special places of worship, perhaps as a calendar or monument to the passage of time and order of the universe.

The shadows created by these communal bonfires served to intensify the images of mystery and imagination; a time to reflect on the passage of life to death, as seen in their lives and crops, a time to imagine their own destinies. This is why they "read" the stars and interpreted their meaning through their stone megaliths, and told their fortunes from the ashes left by the bonfire. Thus *our* Halloween had its roots in this ancient festival, this reflective, introspective, imaginative time at the very beginnings of civilization.

Grotesque stone carving—Notre Dame Cathedral, Paris, France.

The gargoyle, too, which adorns so much medieval and Gothic architecture, is an offshoot of the idea of warding off evil through grotesque replicas of the human head. The gargoyle—the term comes from the Middle English word for throat or "gargle"—was designed to avert evil spirits while clinging to a cathedral's rainspouts, spewing water from its mouth—just as our modern-day jack-o'-lanterns spew smoke to both protect and amuse us.

Unable to eradicate the pagan fascination with grotesque imagery, the early church had become a reluctant party to it.

"What are these fantastic monsters doing in the cloisters under the very eyes of the brothers as they read?" wrote St. Bernard of Clairvaux in the 12th century. "What is the meaning of these unclean monkeys, these savage lions, and monstrous creatures? To what purpose are here placed these creatures, half-beast, half-man, or these spotted tigers?

"I see several bodies with one head, and several heads with one body. Here is a quadruped's head, there again an animal half-horse, half-goat.... Surely if we do not blush from such absurdities, we should at least regret what we have spent on them."

Perhaps what St. Bernard did not understand is that carving grotesque images into any medium—vegetable, stone, wood—evolved from one of earliest man's defense mechanisms. We can only speculate, of course, but it's possible the scenario went something like this:

Before speech, man relied on facial expressions to communicate. Our observant ancestors noticed that animals, particularly large predators, snarled and grimaced to signal not so much their intent to attack, but to warn, to avoid confrontation rather than risk a possibly lethal fight. Thus the *display* of aggression, became the *expression* of aggression, averted aggression itself.

Example of foliating head—stone carving decoration, Yugoslavia.

Nearly all early cultures stylized ferocious imagery, then, in the form of ritual masks to ward off perceived danger or evil, and the masks evolved into the various shapes and forms that have become so much a part of our history and tradition. When the descendants of the ancient Celts emigrated from Scotland and Ireland to the shores of America in the 18th and 19th centuries, they brought with them the custom of carving grotesque faces on turnips. In the New World, though, the turnip gave way to the pumpkin, which was not only plentiful, but easier to work with.

Carvings surrounding a steeple—the medieval version of the junkyard dog, frightening away all evil spirits intent on harm. (Dover, England)

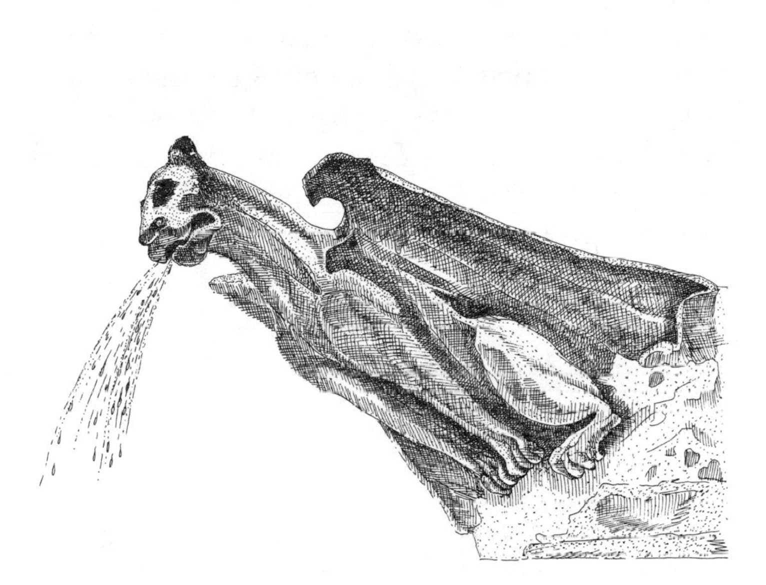

The imaginary Griffin, with the head and body of a lion and the wings of an eagle—Riverside Church, New York City.

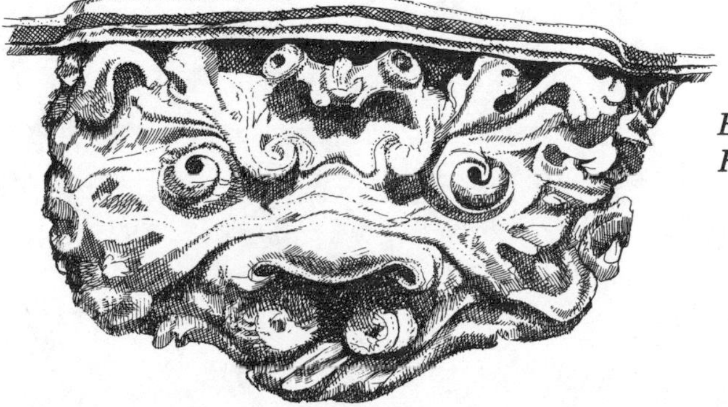

Example of foliating head—Westminster Abbey, Henry VII Chapel wooden decoration.

In order to "rekindle" their ancient practices innocuously, so as not to offend the inhabitants of their newly adopted country, they continued their ancient heritage and had some fun in the process. Only this time, *living through their children*, they had them carry out the "rite of change" for them. Thus the tradition of Halloween has come down to us as a time for children to express themselves creatively.

So from prehistoric man, through the Celtic harvest festival and the Church's establishment in the 7th century of "All-hallows Eve" to honor the souls of the dead, to the shores of the United States, the jack-o'-lantern serves as an annual reminder of what Carl Jung characterized as our collective unconscious, a tradition buried so deep in our past that we can only imagine and wonder at its origins.

The unique imagery of the jack-o'-lantern has come down to us in the form of an amusing character of ourselves; at once us and a thread to the distant past, when men first farmed the land, took a sample of their crops and carved a symbolic image into it, to show their gratitude. Little knowing that the idea would outlast their culture . . . and perhaps ours as well.

CHAPTER TWO • PROCEDURE

Chapter Two: Your Jack-O'-Lantern

A jack-o'-lantern is a vegetable carving that combines image and light, the latter utilized three ways: reflected light from the surface of the carving; generated light from a light bulb or candle that emphasizes the excised features such as eyes, nostrils and mouth; and luminous light that glows eerily through the translucent "skin" of the pumpkin. We turn now to creating this unique form of sculpture.

TOOLS AND DESIGN

You will need a laundry marker, felt pen or crayon to transfer the image you want to create onto the pumpkin's surface. A serrated knife is used to cut the major features and to saw a hole in the top of the pumpkin so the pulp and seeds can be removed. For the actual carving, you will need a ¾-inch-wide wood gouge and a mallet or hammer. These tools do ninety percent of the work.

Once the sculpted image emerges, a potato peeler is used to scrape and model the carved forms to completion. Using the serrated side first, scrape the entire carved surface, then smooth it with the other side.

Round toothpicks are used to hold attachments—eyes, ears, whatever you decide upon—in place. The wood expands in the pumpkin's moist skin and secures the attachments. Glue or metal hairpins will not work.

There are four basic procedures in carving a creative jack-o'-lantern: (1) design, (2) cut, (3) carve, and (4) finish.

You can create a design from your own imagination or borrow one from the comic strips. Any one of your favorite cartoon characters will do. Whether you make a simple line drawing of your own or use a cutout, draw a simple cross over the drawing and a corresponding cross onto the surface (face) of your pumpkin. This cross-grid will allow you to more adequately transfer your idea to sculpture. By observing where each line of your drawing is located on the grid, you can accurately find and transfer the lines of the original to the surface of the pumpkin, copying by the proportion method.

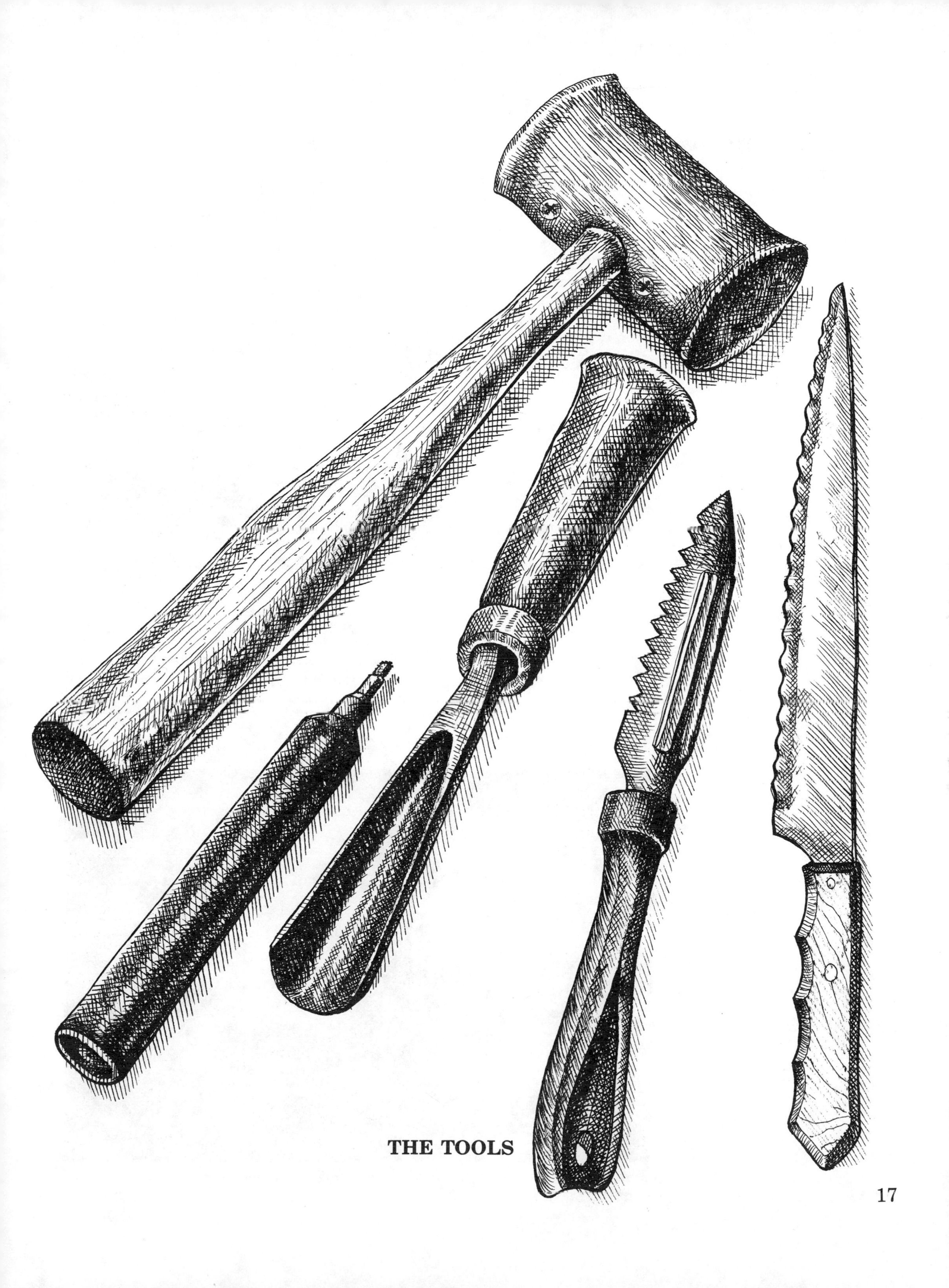

THE TOOLS

THE GRID SYSTEM

(for this stencil see page 55)

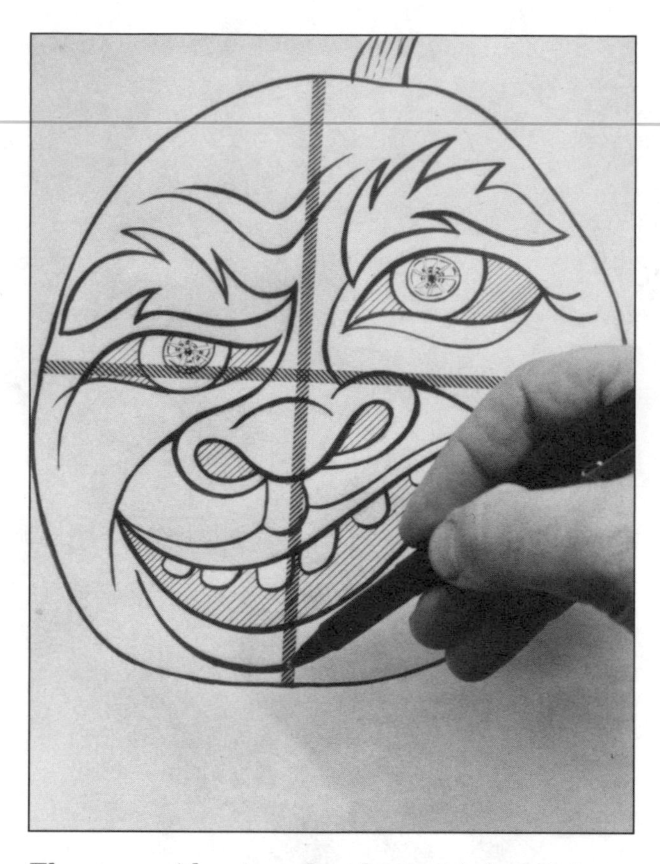

The cross-grid system placed over this brush drawing allows you to transfer it to the pumpkin by the proportion method.

Comparing the drawing with the actual carving; I've eliminated the teeth and changed the expression.

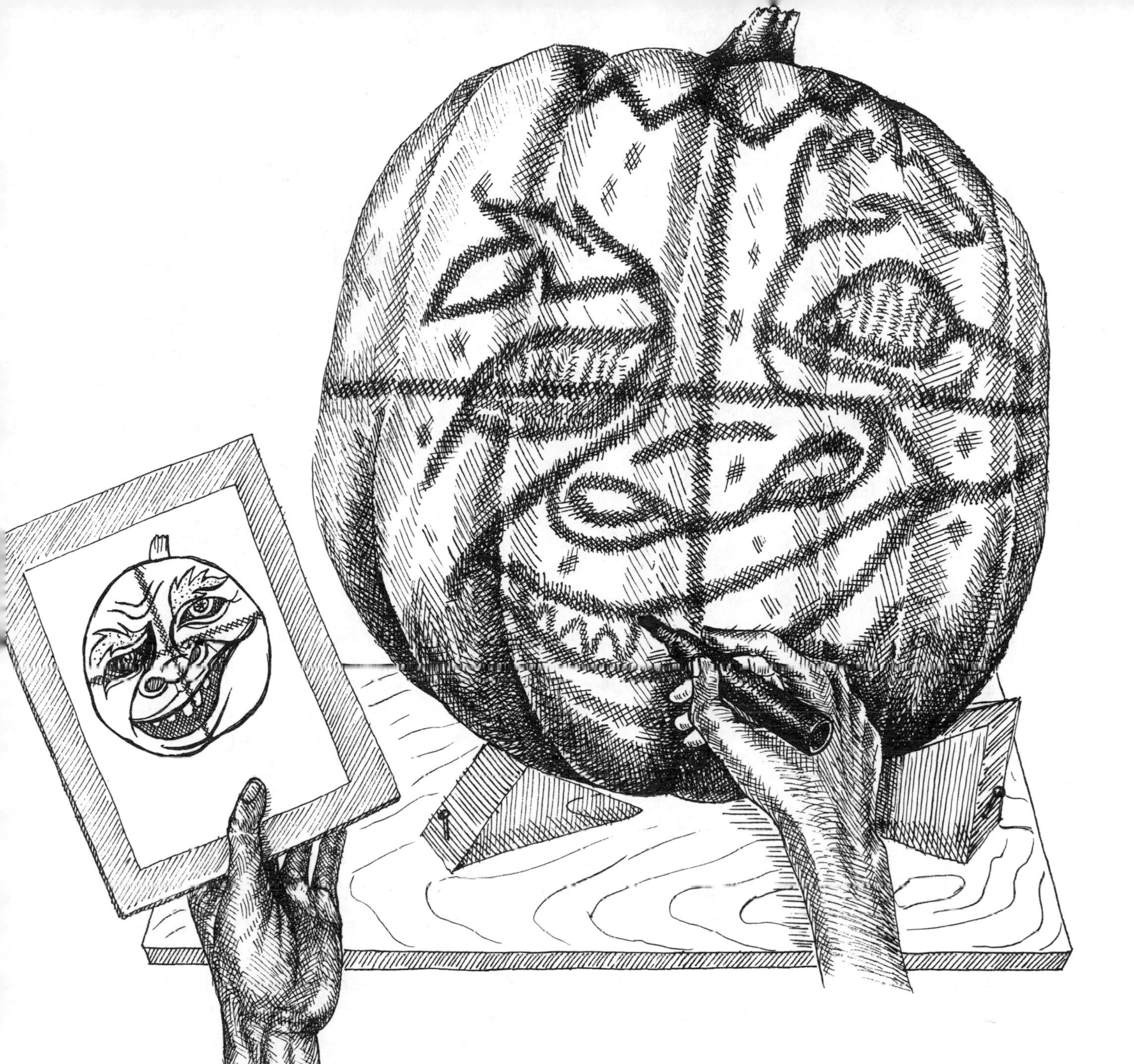

DESIGNING THE PUMPKIN

Before you begin drawing your creation on the pumpkin, you must first make an adequate stand upon which to support your carving. Start with a one-half inch thick plywood stand, and cut several wooden shims or wedges. Set the pumpkin into the desired position, even upside down—whatever position will fit your design. Then nail the wedges to the plywood stand. Use at least three (3) wedges to support the pumpkin, more if it is unusually shaped or very large. Now you're ready to begin the design of the pumpkin; using a laundry marker or crayon, transfer your idea onto the surface of the pumpkin using the grid system, photo-projection or by "eye"—whatever suits you best.

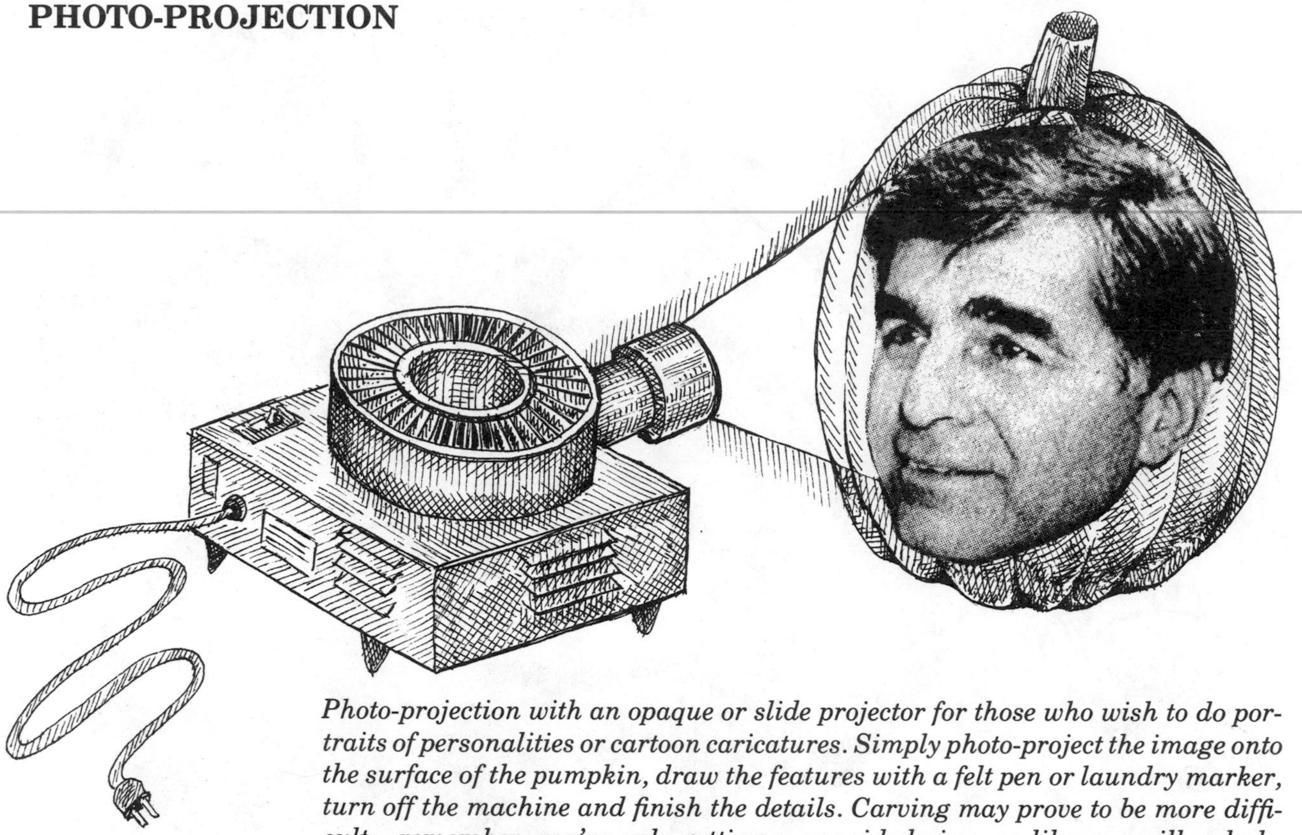

PHOTO-PROJECTION

Photo-projection with an opaque or slide projector for those who wish to do portraits of personalities or cartoon caricatures. Simply photo-project the image onto the surface of the pumpkin, draw the features with a felt pen or laundry marker, turn off the machine and finish the details. Carving may prove to be more difficult—remember, you're only getting a one-sided view, so likeness will only be from that side; as soon as you turn the pumpkin in another direction, you "lose" the likeness.

Another method of transfer is photo-projection. Using an opaque or slide projector, you can transfer an image directly to the surface of the pumpkin while the projector is on and complete the drawing when the projector is turned off. Exact likenesses of personalities are possible using this method, which can be used in stone and wood carving as well.

Once you've transferred your drawing to the pumpkin's surface with a laundry marker, felt pen or crayon, shade or darken the portions which will become the openings, such as the eyes, nostrils and mouth. You will want to save these portions to use later for carved attachments that you can add to your finished jack-o'-lantern.

Use your drawing as a guide rather than as a plan. Drawing is not sculpture. As you begin carving the features, you will see various ways to make your creation more expressive, ways that may, in fact, defy your drawing. In that case, discard the drawing at this point and react to the pumpkin, letting it tell you what it wants you to do. If this sounds familiar, it may be because Michelangelo suggested 400 years ago that a sculptor should let his material tell him what it wants, rather than his being slave to a predetermined plan.

Remember, your audience doesn't know, see or care about your drawing. Only the finished product matters. It will be judged on its creativity, originality and ability to convince. I've often heard from my audiences the reaction, "It looks so real." What they really mean is that the sculptured forms have convinced them. "Looks so real" actually means "good." And when the appreciative viewers reach out to touch your work, you will have been paid the ultimate compliment. Touching verifies existence and indicates you have succeeded in reaching the viewer, affected him or her with your creativity to the point of admiration. And reaching the audience, whether they be two or ninety-two, delighting them with your work, is your goal.

CUTTING THE PUMPKIN

When you're satisfied with the drawing on your pumpkin, I recommend cutting out five openings: two eyes, two nostrils and one large mouth. Using a serrated knife, cut out the shaded portions only, saving them so you can make attachments later for a more creative expressions.

The top portion, and in some cases the bottom portion, of the pumpkin is also removed with a knife, or small handsaw if it is especially thick. Bevel your cuts inward so you can replace the top after the pulp and seeds have been removed.

For younger children, cutting out the openings is the end in itself, inasmuch as they are not yet capable of carving or handling the sharp tools used in the succeeding steps. If careful attention has been paid, though, to making a good preliminary drawing on your pumpkin, the jack-o'-lantern will be a success even without carving it.

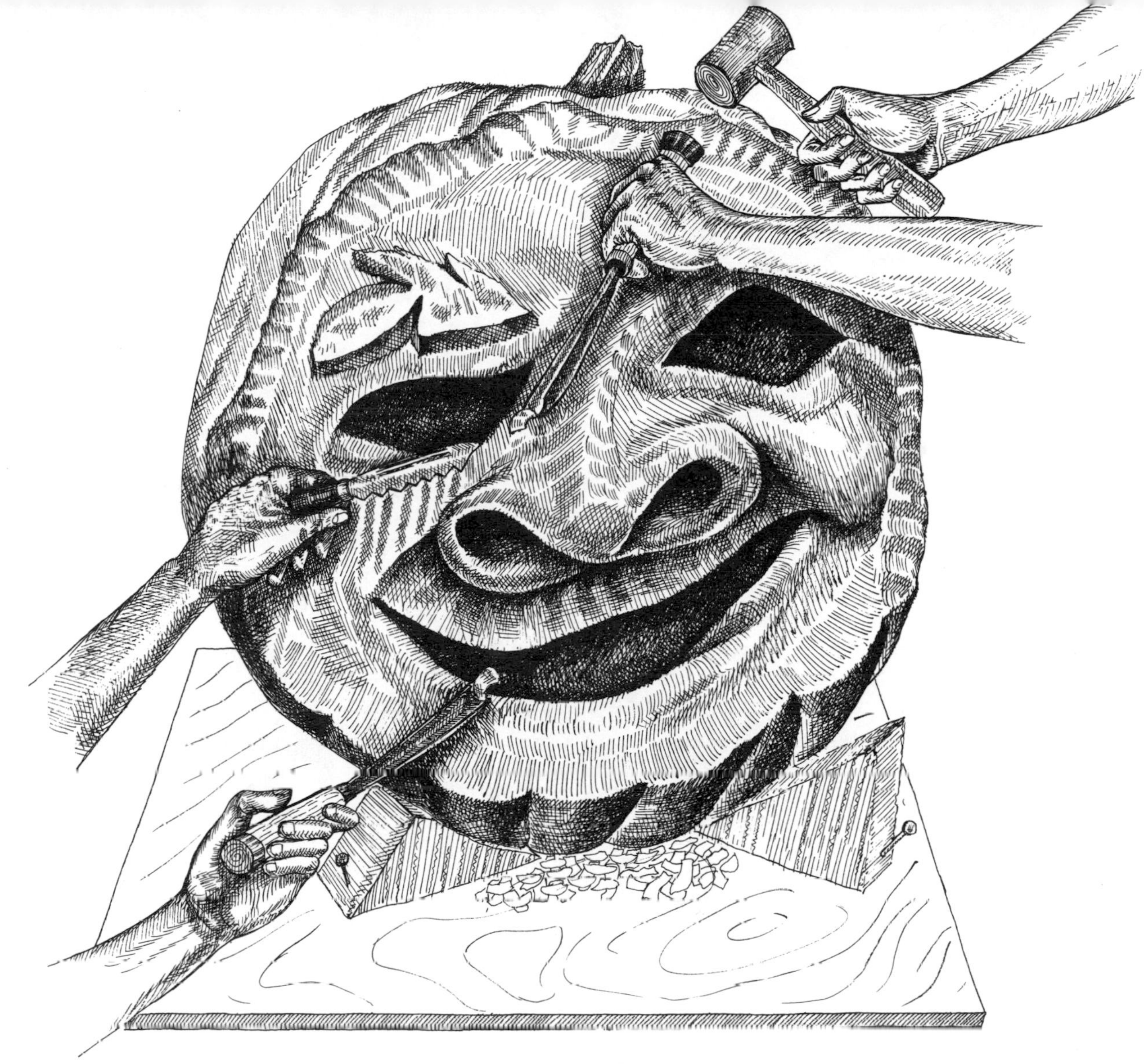

CARVING THE PUMPKIN

Begin carving with a wood gouge and mallet or hammer, starting with the eyes and proceeding to the other cut-out areas, modeling and shaping them so that they begin to look "real." This is where the real artistry begins to take place. Don't be afraid, just plunge right in. If you make a mistake, you can always claim that's what you intended. If you're not into lying, you can repair your error by patching it with a paste made from pumpkin scrapings.

When you can't carve more detail, or when you simply get tired, you can begin to use the serrated side of the potato peeler to scrape away the marks left by the gouge. Scrape in one direction, then cross-scrape, in effect modeling the details so that the carving begins to take on a life of its own. You may want to go back and re-carve some sections to redefine them, then scrape some more and, using the reverse side of the potato peeler, smooth the scrape marks.

If you should break through a section during this process, just take some of the scrapings and plug the hole.

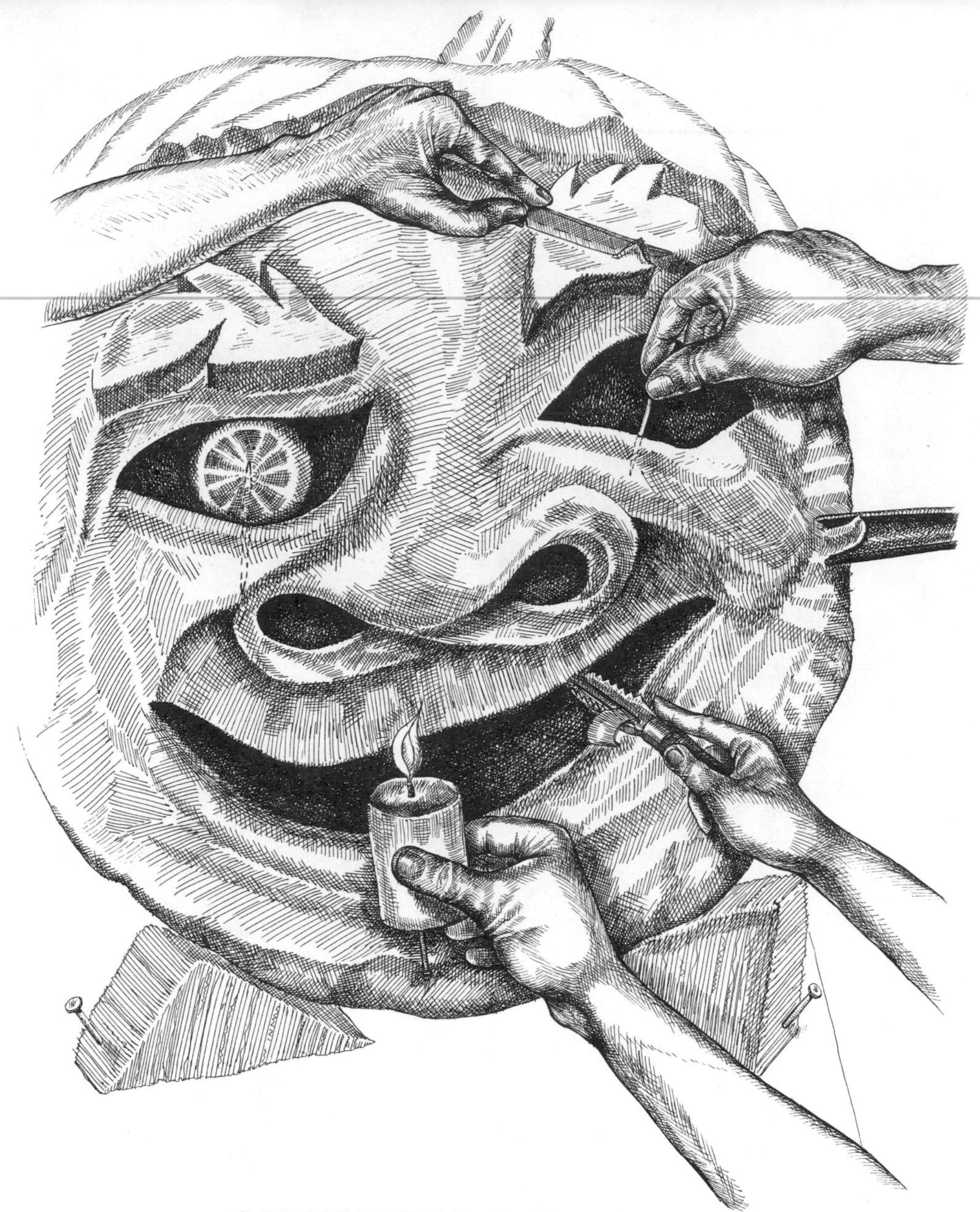

COMPLETING THE DETAILS

Cut the individual shapes of the eyebrows with a small paring knife, which allows you greater flexibility. Press round toothpicks into the bottom portion of the eye-socket, then press on the carved eyeball, gourd or any other vegetable which looks like an eyeball. With a wood gouge carve the "corona" along side the entire face, which will outline and emphasize the details of your carving. Complete your carving with the reverse side of the potato peeler, planing and scraping to satisfaction. To hold the candle firmly in place inside the pumpkin, embed a finish nail into the bottom of the candle and place it into the bottom of the pumpkin before lighting. Leave the wooden shims or wedges nailed to the one-half inch plywood stand in place, covering them with decorative paper or cloth. This will help stabilize your carving, and keep admirers from knocking it over when they reach out to "touch" your work.

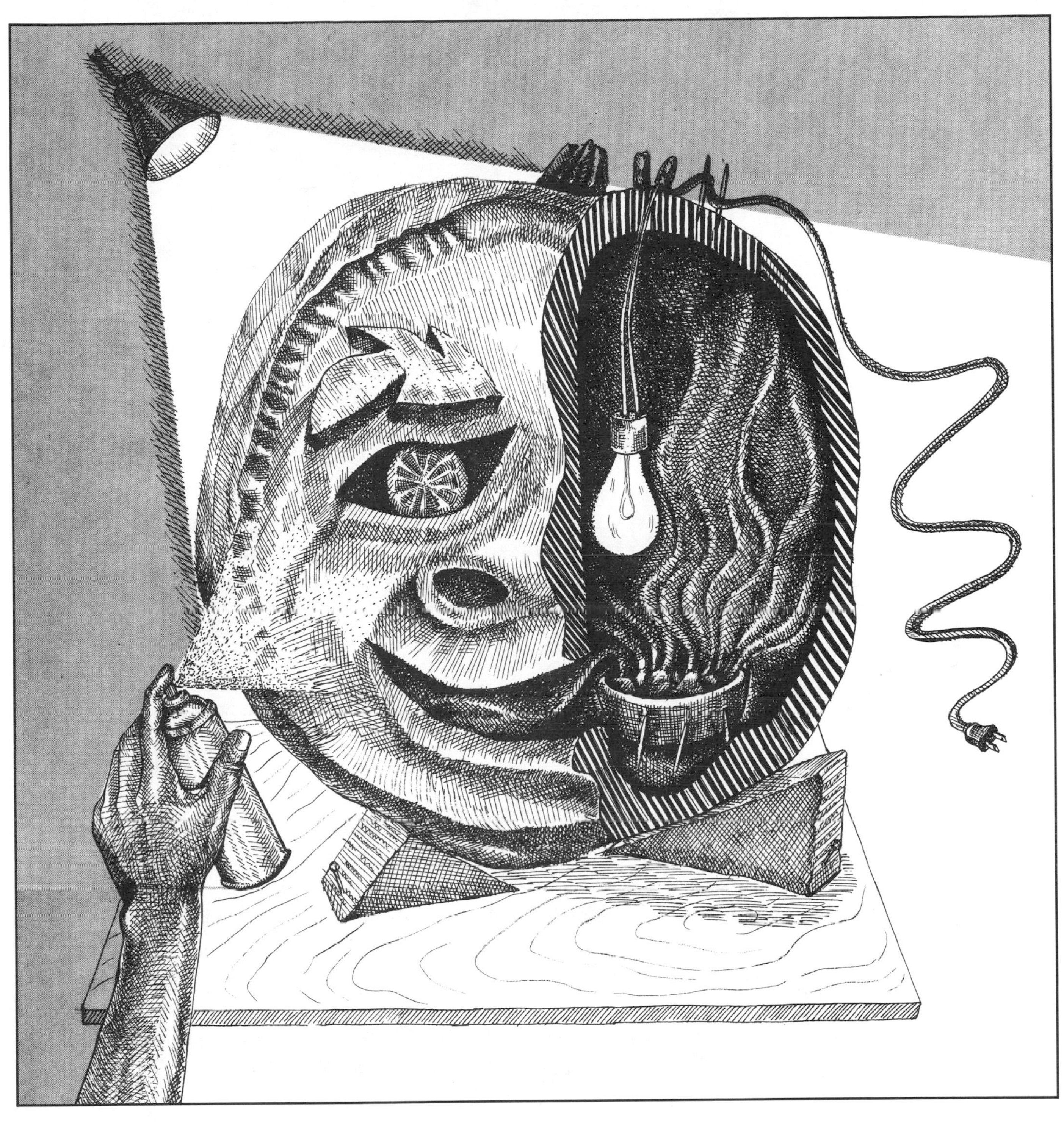

FINISHING YOUR WORK

When you've completed the carving phase, remove the top of your pumpkin with a serrated knife or small hand-saw, beveling the cut inward so you can replace the top after you've removed the contents. In especially large pumpkins, there is little to remove. Your real interest here is to find and save the largest, healthiest seeds for planting, so you can replicate the giant next year. Pulp from smaller pumpkins can be used to make bread or cakes, of course, and it would be a shame to waste it.

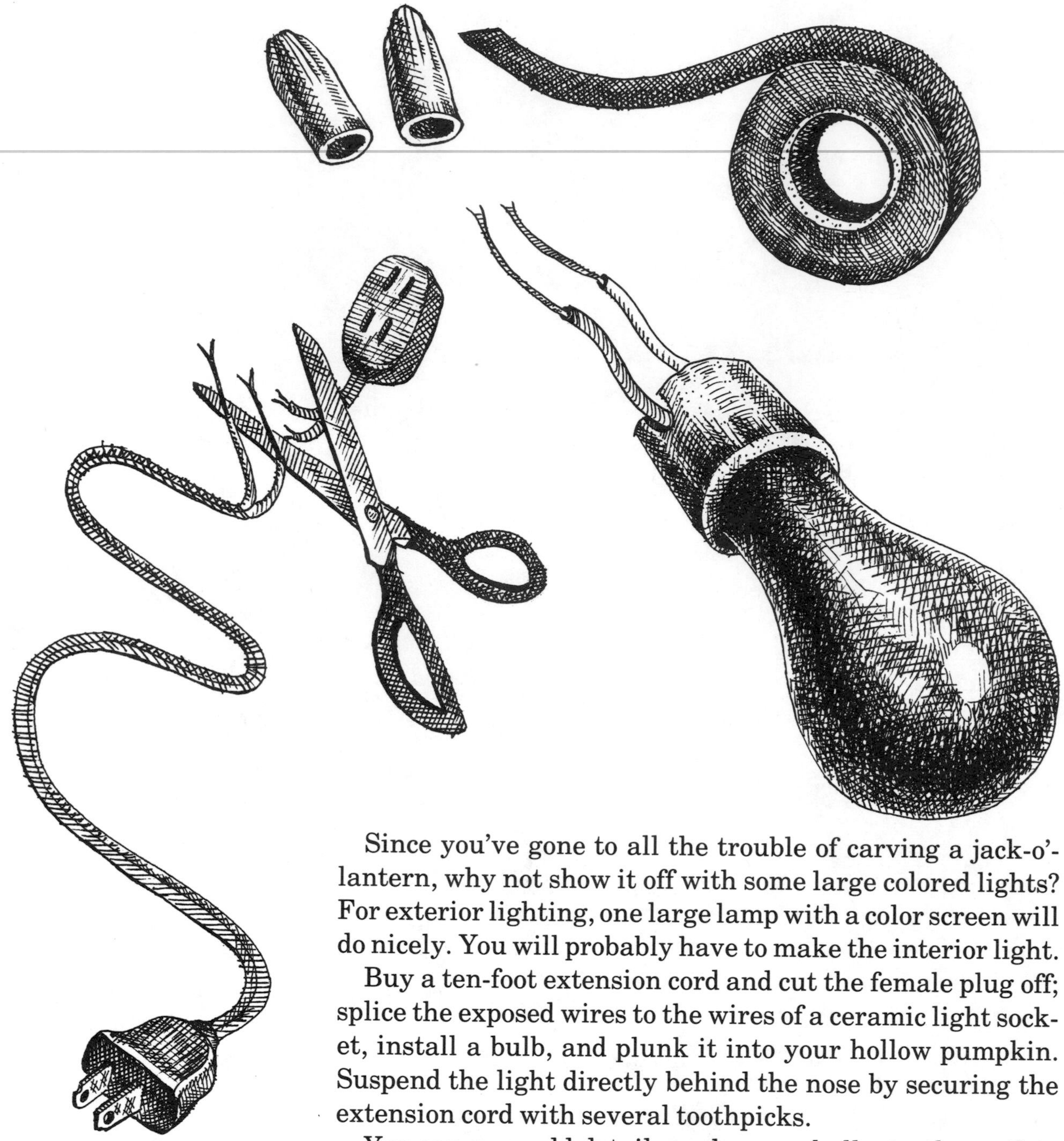

Since you've gone to all the trouble of carving a jack-o'-lantern, why not show it off with some large colored lights? For exterior lighting, one large lamp with a color screen will do nicely. You will probably have to make the interior light.

Buy a ten-foot extension cord and cut the female plug off; splice the exposed wires to the wires of a ceramic light socket, install a bulb, and plunk it into your hollow pumpkin. Suspend the light directly behind the nose by securing the extension cord with several toothpicks.

You can now add details such as eyeballs, teeth or other attachments. These can be the pieces cut from your pumpkin or miniature squash. In either case, remember to use wooden toothpicks.

When the details and features are placed to your satisfaction, spray your creation with lacquer. Give it several coats, both inside and outside, allowing each coat to dry before applying the next one. Any spray fixative, the kind used on drawings, or hair spray, will work. The lacquer gives your jack-o'-lantern a glossy appearance, enhances the details, and preserves it for at least a week by sealing the surface and holding the moisture.

A word of caution. Read the label before applying anything to the surface of your pumpkin. Toxics should be avoided for the obvious reason: curious small children will want, and should be encouraged, to touch the finished product of your creation.

SPECIAL EFFECTS

I recommend using a red 25-watt bulb rather than the traditional candle in your jack-o'-lantern. For one thing, fire codes prohibit open flame if you exhibit your work in public places. The electric light, too, is brighter and lends to the luminosity effect I spoke of earlier, whereas a flickering candle is often difficult to see.

A small bowl of warm water into which you immerse cubes of dry ice will emulate that smoky, eerie effect to typical of Halloweens. The only problem here is that you will have to continually replenish the dry ice and warm water to duplicate the effect. An overhead colored light will illuminate the "smoke" (dry ice fumes) as it emanates from the openings in the pumpkin.

If you want to create the gargoyle effect, though, I recommend that you rent a fogging machine. This machine is nothing more than a container holding warm water and a cake of dry ice. A fan draws the fumes through a hose and into the pumpkin. The result is a spectacle to behold. "Smoke" billows from the nostrils and mouth of the jack-o'-lantern, catching the red light inside, the colored light outside, and imitating the rainwater spewing from the mouths of gargoyles atop the great cathedrals. The dramatic effect is a sure crowd-pleaser and the highlight of any demonstration. When children rush up to wave their hands through the "smoke" and shriek with delight, you will know your efforts were well worth it.

THE GARGOYLE EFFECT

CHAPTER THREE • RESULTS

Chapter 3: The Giant Pumpkins

This chapter is for those who feel confident enough to attempt carving the giant pumpkins, those ranging from 300 pounds to more than 600 pounds. It sometimes takes several men or even a tractor to move them. The carving method is similar to that used on the smaller pumpkins, but you may want to use special gouges to do the work faster. Only practice and experience, though, will enable you to carve the giants better.

Getting a giant pumpkin isn't easy, but it is possible. You can grow your own by purchasing hybrid seeds available through any of the large seed catalogue houses and many nurseries. Or you can have a gardening enthusiast grow one for you. As a last resort, watch your local supermarket, where area growers may bring especially large pumpkins for display.

Keep in mind that the larger and rounder the pumpkin, the more character you can carve into its soft, pulpy surface. Notice that I said *round*. Some pumpkins have a tendency to grow flat, and these odd-shaped ones don't look enough like a human head to create an effective expression.

CARVING THE FEATURES

As with the smaller pumpkins, once you've settled on a design that you like, and one that will delight your audience, draw it onto the surface of the giant and shade the areas to be cut out, then cut with a knife or hand-saw, whichever is easier.

Carving the details can be very time consuming and difficult. Often when I'm performing a demonstration, the audience wants to see something fast, as though I were some sort of magician, or the local television crew wants a fast take and will ask me to "hurry it up." I don't see any harm in hurring it up—as long as I can go back to doing it right once they leave.

To demonstrate how thick the giant pumpkin is, and to convince the audience that it is indeed a real pumpkin, I usually leave the eyebrows intact. And I make a corona around the face, leaving the marks made by the wood gouge. The wrinkles and grooves in the face are created first with a knife, then later with a potato peeler, using the end like a knife but scraping rather than cutting.

When you think you've finished carving, you can begin to scrape with the peeler, using the serrated side first, then cross-scraping, and finally smoothing the surface with the reverse side. With a large pumpkin, you may have to go back to carving several times before you achieve the proper form and the "real" look.

In this street fair carving we see the initial phases of the carving process, noting the deepest parts are carved first.

Cutting the top out of a large pumpkin can be a chore. Sometimes a small hand-saw is necessary due to the extreme thickness, which can exceed nine inches.

One of the growers is cleaning out his pumpkin, keeping the largest and healthiest seeds so that he can grow another giant next year.

FACIAL FEATURES

The quality of your jack-o'-lantern will depend on how inventive you are with its features. The eyes especially lend emotion, the nose character, and the mouth expression.

Speaking of the mouth, pointed, canine-type teeth tend to frighten smaller children. Square, "dumb looking" teeth, on the other hand, may be OK, but I tend to avoid them altogether because I can gain more expression from the shape of the lips and subtle detail around them than I can get from teeth. Besides, the "dental work" blocks the dry ice "smoke" during the gargoyle phase of my demonstration.

Instead of carving a section of pumpkin for the jack-o'-lantern's eyes, I've lately been using gourds, which look almost exactly like human eyes. Miniature pumpkins and unusually shaped gourds can also be used as attachments. One attachment I don't do is ears. Being a "pumpkin purist," I refuse to add attachments that look ridiculous—or can and will be pulled off by small children.

Throughout the years, I've tried many types and shapes of jack-o'-lanterns. I've discovered that one-eyed monsters or strange, contorted sculptures, while they may amuse an audience, are inherently weak. The audience senses something is missing. I suspect what's missing is that image we carry in our collective subconscious of pumpkin-turned-man, that image of the primeval lantern/mask. So as an artist, I follow my historic orders and try as best I can to interpret and re-create that subliminal image.

This jack-o'-lantern was carved in about four hours. I try to emphasize the difference in each side of the face, which in this case was inspired by my ex-mother-in-law. Nothing is more boring than sculpting a duplicate pattern for each side of the face.

This close-up version shows us the final surface of the completed carving; the tool marks of the potato peeler, the original skin of the eyebrows, the smooth surface of the nostrils, and the three toothpicks holding the miniature gourd, which looks just like an eyeball. The whole pumpkin is, in fact, a ready-made mask just waiting to be carved—all you have to do is complete the features.

DEMONSTRATION AND PARTICIPATION

Demonstrating jack-o'-lantern carving at shopping malls and pumpkin festivals gives the public access to your ideas and gives them ideas of their own about how to carve pumpkins. Children of all ages enjoy seeing how it's done. Colored lights, black backdrops (the better to see the color and fog), and the huge pumpkin propped on a wooden stand three feet from the ground will all enhance your exhibit. Cornstalks, hay or straw, and other props will help convey the harvest theme.

Still untried is placing a microphone inside the pumpkin, so that someone near the jack-o'-lantern could actually talk to the children and answer their questions.

I usually ask children—and adults, for that matter—to step up and touch the jack-o'-lantern while I'm still carving it. This eases the children's apprehensions and gives their parents an opportunity to take a picture of them (in costume) next to the great pumpkin. By asking the audience to participate in the creation, I preserve and perpetuate the moment. The pumpkin itself may last only about a week before it turns to mush, but the touching and the photographs establish a timeless link between idea and audience. A uniquely American folk art tradition is carried on to another generation.

Make every effort, then, to make your presentation as interesting and meaningful as possible.

The stand which supports this jack-o'-lantern is wide enough to accommodate this child. This enables me to set aside my carving tools so that parents can take pictures of their costumed children next to the jack-o'-lantern.

Occasionally guests are invited to help me carve the jack-o'-lantern. It is a means of getting the audience to participate in the act of sculpture. Note the direction of the gouge marks in the carving process.

Supermarkets are ideal places to demonstrate your pumpkin carving skills; you have a captive audience of onlookers, and the grocers will love you.

This carving demonstrates the real purpose of the openings for eyes, nostrils and mouth. The black curtain in the background helps emphasize the dry-ice fumes, which are highlighted by the exterior colored lights.

Young children enjoy running through the dry-ice vapors emanating from the jack-o'-lantern, which becomes the highlight of the show. Spacing your demonstrations every twenty minutes will conserve the amount of dry ice needed for the demonstration.

THE ART OF TEACHING ART

As a teaching tool for getting students involved with the art of sculpture and the discipline of carving, pumpkin carving is probably the easiest and most convenient. Most colleges and universities have beginning sculpture programs that first introduce the students to a variety of disciplines: modeling clay, carving wood and stone, and welding metal.

About the time the instructors have finished presenting the clay modeling segment of the course, they begin teaching wood carving. The students seek out a chunk of wood, usually a log, and proceed to butcher it, ruining their tools and understanding little in the process. Carving is difficult for the novice, and unless one is dedicated to it, not much is learned—except frustration.

A better way, I believe, to acquaint the students with carving is to have them carve a pumpkin. The soft, pulpy texture is easy to work with—and easy on carving tools—the base material is readily available, and within a short time, the end product is ready for "exhibit" and public appreciation. If the student then wishes to proceed to wood carving, he or she will be more aware of how to use tools and less intimidated by difficulty.

At the junior and senior high school levels, students approach pumpkin carving with relish, though janitors are usually less enthusiastic. At these grade levels, students are eager to work in groups where they can chit-chat and share tools and discoveries about method. Speaking of tools, I've had students who substituted spoons for gouges and shared pocket knives, even toothpicks. The most expensive item in the project was the pumpkin.

At the lower grade levels, I recommend a slight change in the procedures. Younger students have neither the patience nor the coordination to completely carve a pumpkin. Gather them in groups of three to five and lay a large piece of plastic sheeting on the floor. Have the children sit in a circle and encourage them to cut, rather than carve, their pumpkins. A small, blunt hand saw will do, or a special pumpkin knife.

The teacher's duty here is to show the students how to work from drawings by transferring the designs to the pumpkins, then encouraging the youngsters to work from the two-dimensional to the three-dimensional. When they have finished, line the jack-o'-lanterns up and ask the students to choose the best or the funniest of the bunch. By working together and sharing and comparing the experience of creation, these students won't need any prodding when it comes time for next year's jack-o'-lantern parade.

Young children are encouraged to touch the carving. Sometimes shy children are afraid, but with a little coaching from their parents, their anxieties can be overcome.

A librarian completes a display in the children's section of the library, complete with cornstalks, bales of hay and Halloween backdrops to enhance the display. It also helps children remember the idea.

Children are encouraged to touch the "great pumpkin." They seem to delight in reacting with the jack-o'-lantern during this "Gargoyle" phase, when smoke instead of rainwater spews from their mouths.

The opening for the mouth was so large that it collapsed onto itself, but did offer me an opportunity to develop the lips. Remember, the larger the pumpkin, the more character can be carved into it.

The glow given off by this carving is from a 25-watt light bulb suspended from the top opening; the bulb's intensity is far greater than the light of a candle.

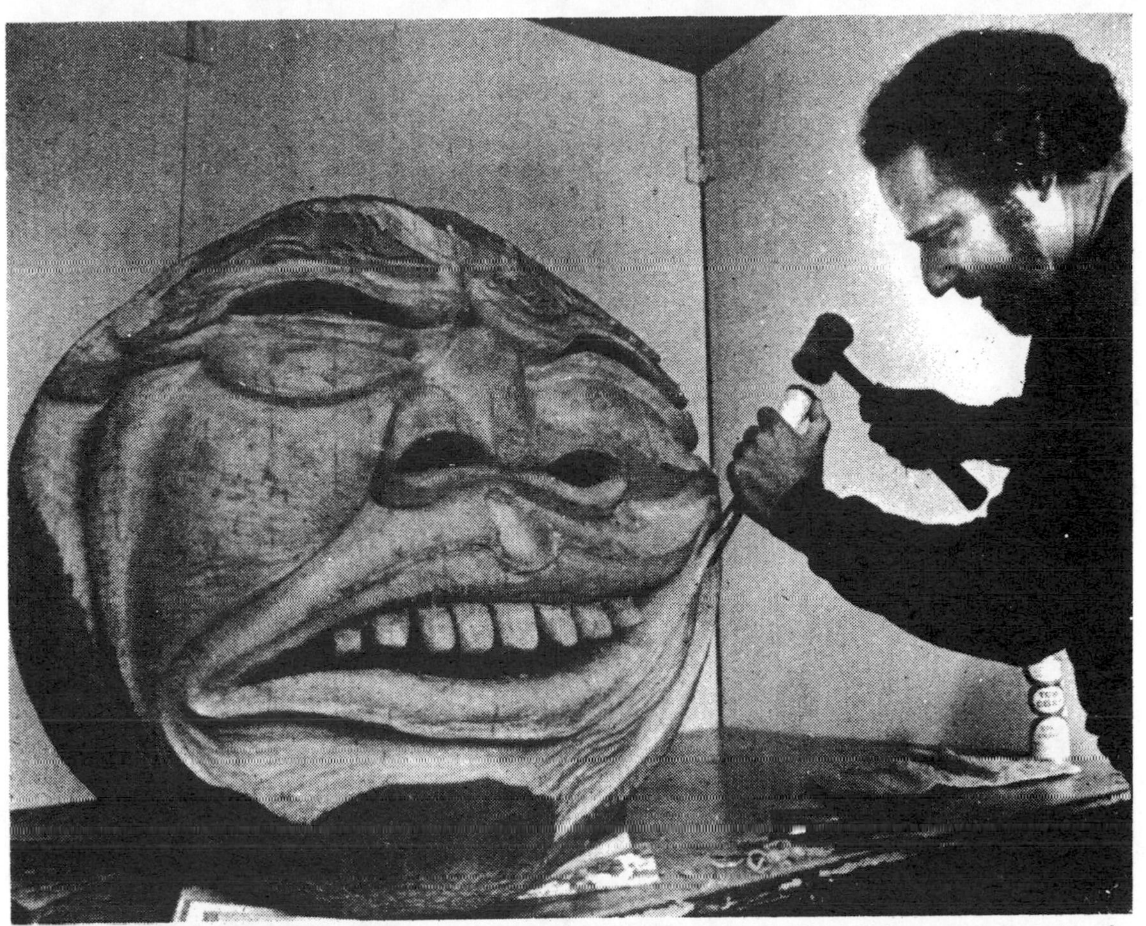

Here the author poses with two of his earlier "dental" versions. Teeth will keep your creation from collapsing onto itself, but does limit the flow of dry-ice fumes.

Here the author is cleaning out a 200-pound creation. Toothpicks were used to hold up the lips, which after carving immediately began to collapse. Note the thickness of the cut-out top. A full set of teeth might have prevented this problem.

This 310-pound giant had an especially wide shape, which enabled me to emphasize the cheeks and lips; the drawing on the eyebrows was left because it looked so much like hair.

This somewhat flattened pumpkin offered me the opportunity of utilizing the cheeks and mouth for expression. Note that the right side of the face is completely different than the left side; this difference helps emphasize the character of the jack-o'-lantern.

FOR PARENTS AND PRE-SCHOOLERS

Some children, particularly young children, have difficulty in creating an original idea for their jack-o'-lantern, and for that matter so do their parents and teachers. Instead of creating, they ramble, or simply do not possess the mechanical ability to draw or carve. In this case, I recommend using the *jack-o'-lantern stencils* on the preceding pages. I have designed five stencils especially for this purpose; stencils #1, #2 and #3 are simple cut-outs, whereas #4 and #5 are for more advanced students using larger pumpkins. The stencils solve the creative and mechanical problems, freeing the children to have some fun creating and exhibiting something they can do with their own hands. Further, these children develop their own eye/hand coordination and learn something about the art of sculpture. After all, you can buy plans to build a piece of furniture or a house, why should carving a jack-o'-lantern be any different?

How to use the stencils:

1. Cut the preferred drawing out of the book with a scissors (for parents or teachers only).

2. Cut out the black portions of the stencil with a matt knife, using a full newspaper for backing. Save the cut-out pieces for another pumpkin. Again this is an exercise for adults.

3. Tape the stencil to the pumpkin and fill in the cut-outs with a laundry marker, crayon or, if you're in a hurry, a can of colored spray paint.

4. Remove the stencil and begin to cut the outline you made over the stencil. Use a blunt knife or small saw to carve your pumpkin. Just show the child how to cut, and let them proceed with the rest of the pumpkin.

5. With a potato peeler, scrape the areas shown on the drawing with striated lines, such as the lips and brow. This will add texture to your carving.

6. Cut small sections of pumpkin from the scraps to create the eyeballs; they can be any shape you choose, or even another vegetable. Simply embed a round toothpick into them, and stick them into the eye socket.

7. Save the cut-out sections from the stencil (the black areas) which can now be taped to another pumpkin and arranged in *any* fashion on *any* sized pumpkin. You and your child can make up interesting versions of a jack-o'-lantern, taping the cut-out sections anywhere on the pumpkin, until you settle on a design that meets with your child's approval. Merely cut around the taped portions with a knife, modelling and rounding off the cut-out design with the serrated end of the potato peeler.

8. Finally, cut out the top, remove the seeds, place a candle inside, and your child has created a jack-o'-lantern. Save the stencil and cut-outs for next year.

Stencils #4 and #5 were designed for larger pumpkins which would be fully carved; that's why the eyebrows should be treated like the carving on the cover. Remember, these stencils are intended as suggestions for a creative idea; if you feel that they could be made better, by all means, change them to accommodate your own creativity. Happy carving!

For Stencils #1 & #2

For Stencils #3 & #4

INSTRUCTIONS

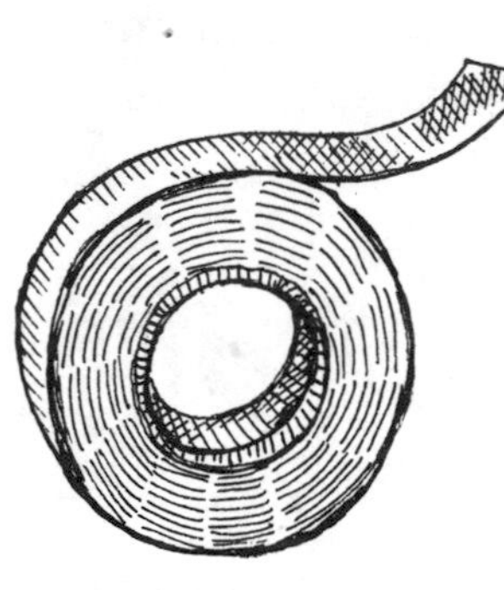

TOOLS

1) "*Quik-Karve*": a pumpkin carving knive, designed especially for children, features no sharp edges and rounded safety tip.
2) *Potato peeler*: for rounding and modifying openings.
3) *Laundry marker or crayon*: to mark openings, or carve directly into the surface with the pumpkin knife.
4) *Tape*: to hold the jack-o-lantern stencil to the pumpkin.
5) *Toothpicks*: the rounded type to secure the eyeballs and other attachments.

For all stencil cutouts

The jack-o'-lantern stencils offer the convenience of working from a set of plans. This is especially important for young children first getting into the act of carving a jack-o'-lantern. Let them do as much of the work as possible.

JACK-O'-LANTERN STENCIL #1

JACK-O'-LANTERN STENCIL #2

JACK-O'-LANTERN STENCIL #3

JACK-O'-LANTERN STENCIL #4

JACK-O'-LANTERN STENCIL #5

DIRECTIONS

1. *Cut two pages out of book with scissors.*
2. *Tape two pages together.*
3. *Cut out black areas with mat knife.*
4. *Tape to surface of pumpkin and mark cut-out areas.*
5. *Cut out areas with knife.*
6. *Find lines on drawing by making pin holes and extend lines off the drawing.*
7. *Carve and finish to satisfaction.*

CHAPTER FOUR • GROWING

Chapter 4: Growing Pumpkins

The pumpkin's capacity to imitate the size and shape of the human head has endeared it to many cultures. In the American Southwest, preserved pumpkin seeds have been dated to 15,000 years ago. In Indochina, mythology traces the origin of the inhabitants to a race of pumpkins, and jack-o'-lanterns are still a large part of the cultural tradition in that part of the world. Hollow vegetables—pumpkins and squash—have been food sources, symbols, even toys, for as long as man can remember—and longer. The pumpkin's bright orange represents the full bloom of life and the maturity celebrated by the harvest festival. And the blacks of the carved jack-o'-lanterns are mute symbols of the more sinister origins of Halloween.

Every October, grocery stores throughout the nation stock vast quantities of pumpkins, not to *eat*, but to *carve*. Our beloved "pumpkin" pie, by the way, is made primarily of squash. So we have done what every society before us has done, relegated the pumpkin to ceremony and the traditions of folk art. And in America, land of the superlatives, we naturally had to make it bigger and better—at least bigger.

Commercial farmers and garden enthusiasts have competed for years to produce the largest and most spectacular pumpkins for exhibit at county fairs and harvest festivals. But in recent years a new kind of festival has gained in popularity—the pumpkin festival.

The pumpkin festival is a response to growers eager to exhibit their wares—and to the fair organizers' efforts to promote their communities. *Size* is the watchword. While the giant hybrid pumpkins have been around for at least thirty years, several new breeds are now growing to incredible proportions, in many cases more than 600 pounds in a single, seven-month growing period. With intensive competition, the lure of prize money, and the promise of fame, growers assure us their pumpkins will grow even larger. But how do you get started on this road to fame and fortune? Where do you buy the seeds, and what do you do with them once you have them?

The selection process begins, checking for the largest, roundest and most rot-free pumpkin in the patch. Note the amount and size of the leaves needed to support these giants. This variety of pumpkin is low on acreage but spectacular in size. From a single seed, this grower realized 1100 pounds of pumpkin; if this gardener had pruned this plant instead of allowing all five pumpkins to grow from it, he would have had a record 500- or 600-pound pumpkin.

"Grunting" it off the tractor bucket, we were surprised to find that it only weighed 310 pounds. Their size, cumbersome shape and field conditions dictate the use of a tractor to remove them from the field.

As noted earlier, special hybrid seeds are available from many nurseries and seed companies. You can also get them at pumpkin festivals through barter or by purchasing seeds from the prize-winners. As you can imagine, these seeds aren't cheap, but for a nominal outlay of a dollar per seed, you can at least begin your efforts to grow a giant pumpkin.

Once you have your precious seeds in hand, don't wash them. Allow them to dry naturally, then wrap them in something that will permit them to breathe, such as cloth or paper towels. Don't wrap your seeds in plastic or put them in a glass jar. Both will retain moisture and encourage fungus growth, which will render your seeds worthless. Store your properly wrapped seeds in a dark place, and forget about them until spring.

March is the time to prepare for planting. Soak the seeds first, then plant them directly, pointed end down, in conditioned soil. Some growers like to start seedlings indoors then transplant them. The problem with this is the seedlings often appear to go into shock and die within a week after transplanting. I have heard that "sun shock" can be avoided by permitting the seedlings to sunbathe gradually before transplanting. Possibly. But my experience has been that even then the transplants die or grow very little. Worse, bugs and other predators seem to sense the transplanted seedling is weak and does not belong, so they do what they were designed to do—they devour the plant.

To avoid these problems, then, I suggest planting your expensive seed directly into prepared soil where it will be protected from frost, sun and pests. See the accompanying illustrations for further information about growing giant pumpkins. Your pumpkins should be ready for harvest by mid-October, just in time for festival weigh-ins.

7 MONTHS GROWING SEASON
(MARCH TO OCTOBER)

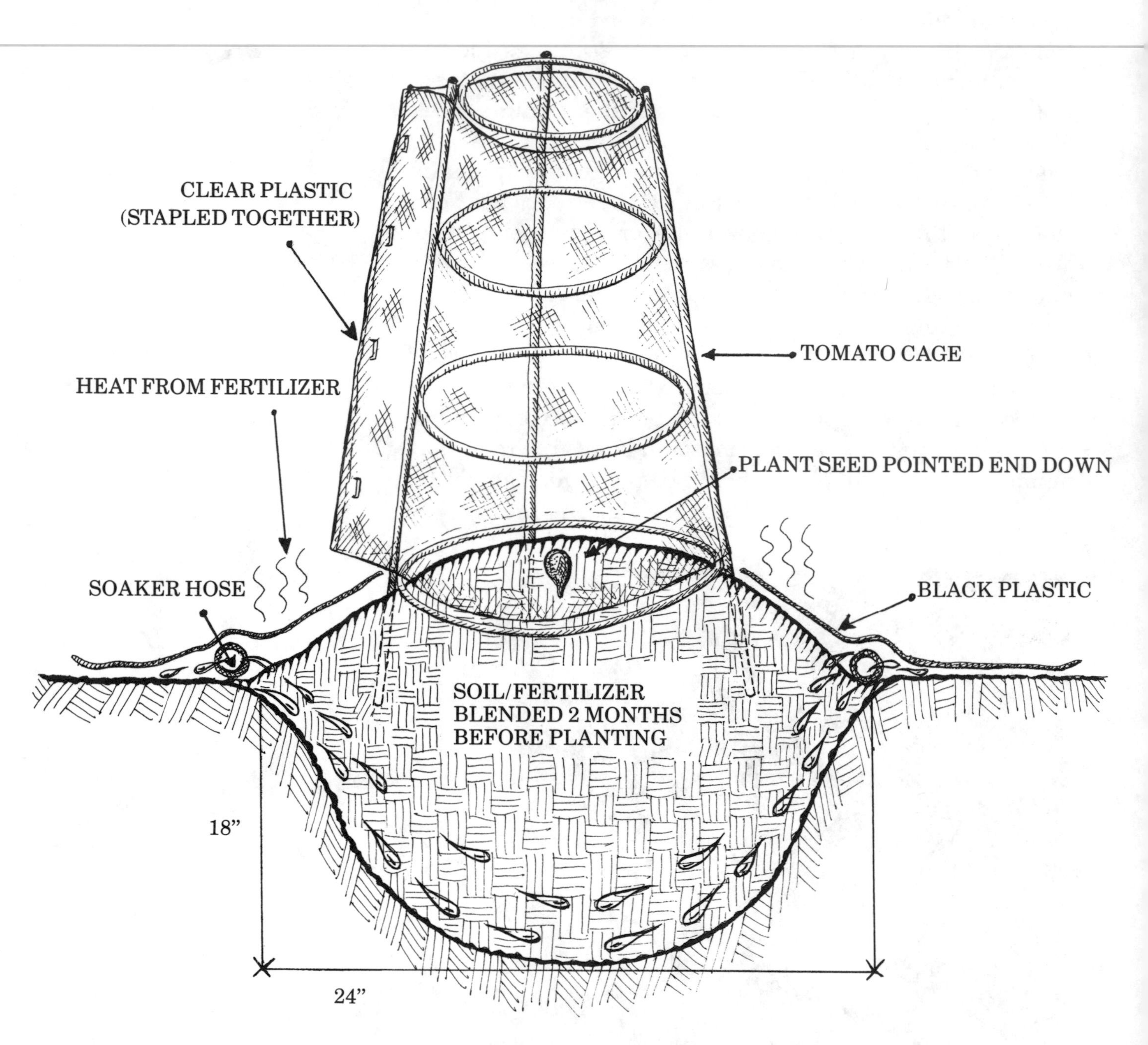

GROWING GIANT PUMPKINS

In March, plant your special hybrid seed, pointed end down, in a specially prepared soil-fertilizer mixture that has had about two months to "work." Heat generated by the fertilizer should warm the soil sufficiently so the seed can withstand a freeze, and a tomato cage wrapped with clear plastic will serve as added insurance. As the summer months approach, encircle the mound of soil with a soaker hose. Black plastic over the prepared soil preserves moisture and will keep the plant from drying out. Pumpkins are the hogs of the vegetable world, so feed them plenty of water, occasional plant food, and milk.

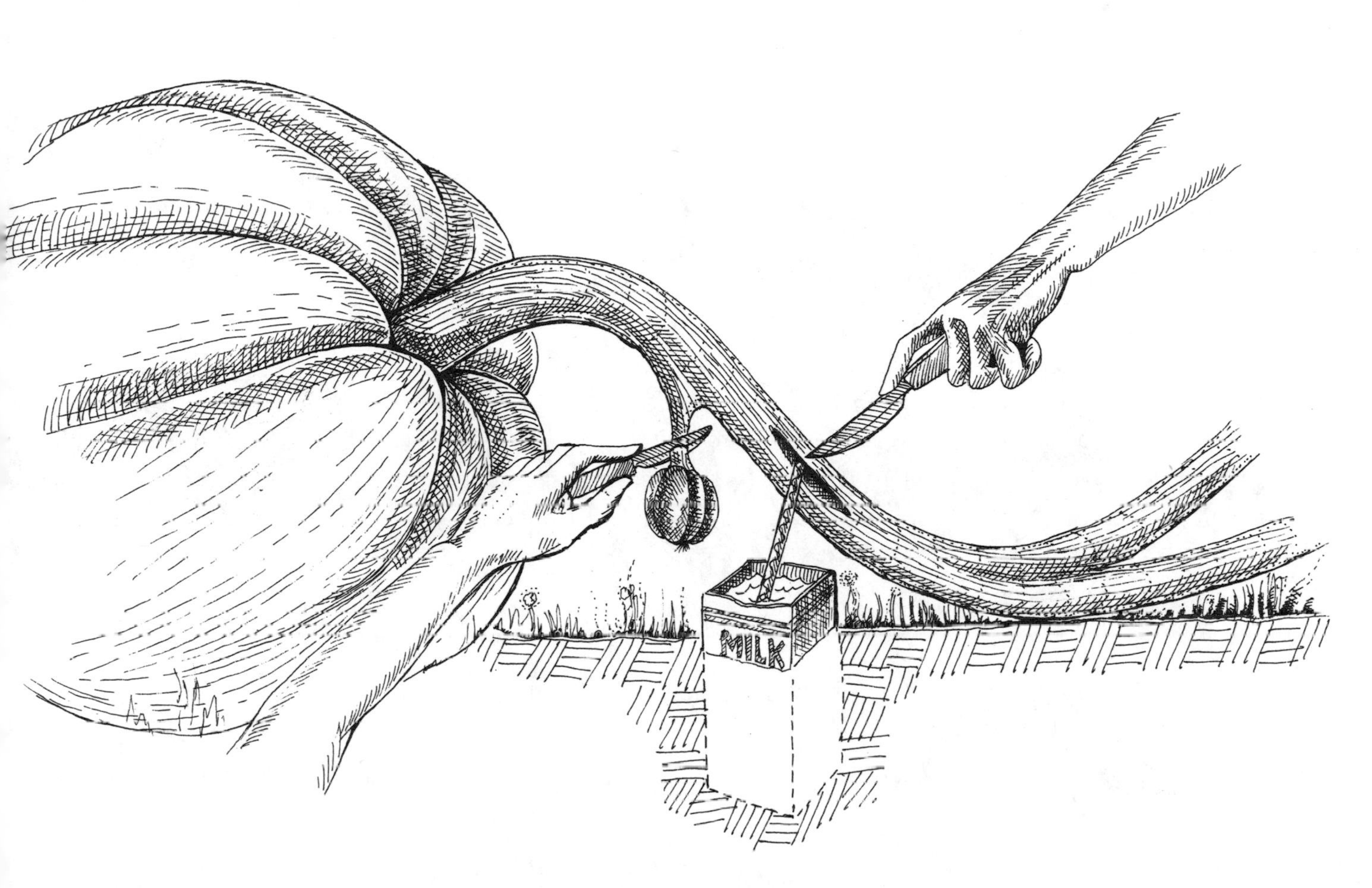

MILK FEEDING

To increase the size of your pumpkin, you might consider feeding it milk or sugar water during the last two weeks of growth. Simply cut a 2-inch-wide by ¼-inch-deep slice in the pumpkin's major vine. Insert a cloth wick or some other absorbent material and connect it to the half-buried milk carton. You have then created a secondary vine, and the pumpkin will draw extra nutrition from it. Periodically turning your pumpkin, being careful not to damage the vine, will help keep your pumpkin round. To further enhance growth, remove any fruit from the plant that will rob your "giant" pumpkin of nutrition.

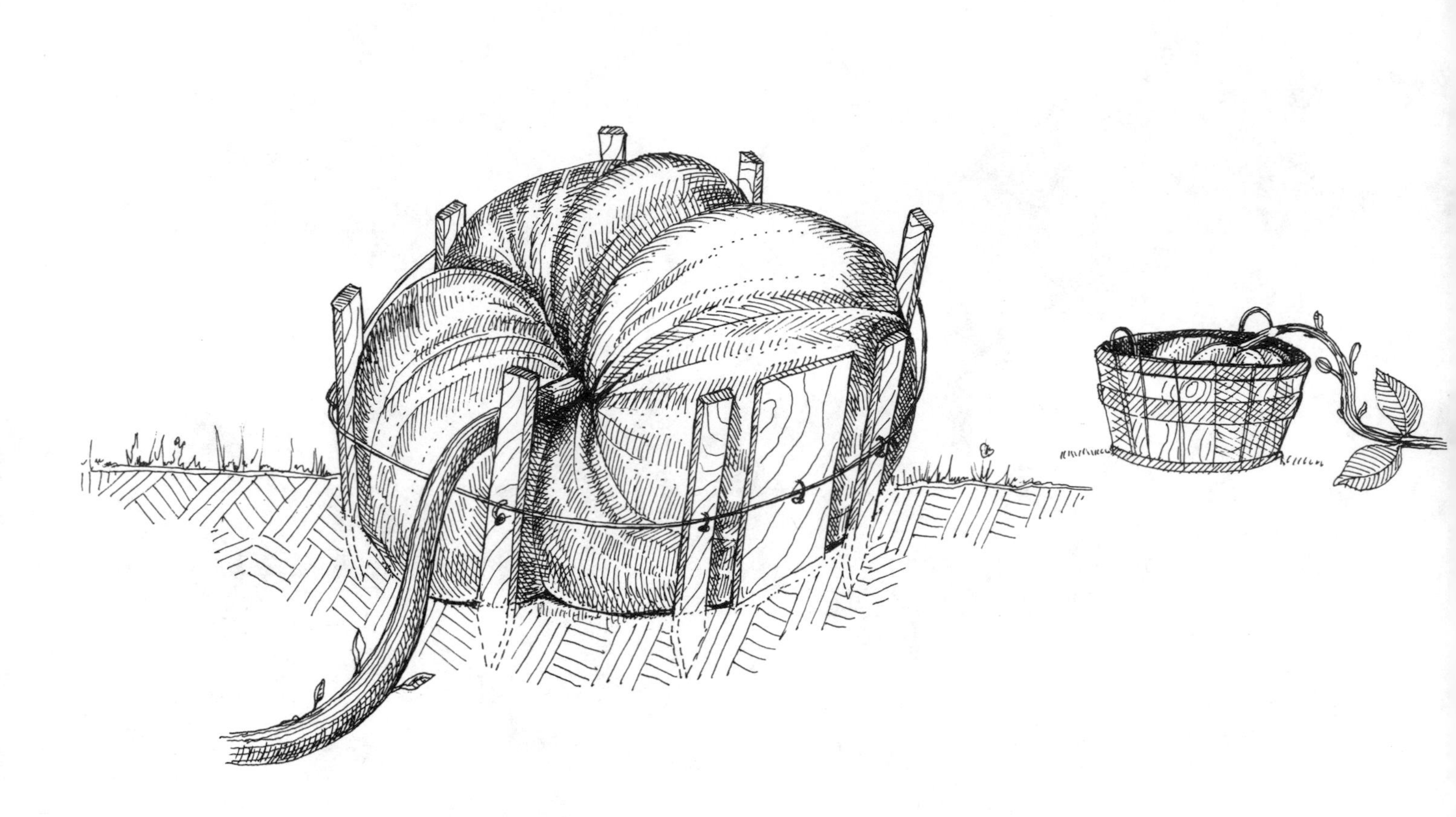

Giant pumpkins do not always grow round. Sometimes they grow as flat as pancakes. In order to avoid the "pancake syndrome," I recommend building a wooden stake fence around your half-grown pumpkin, or placing it in a bushel basket. This will encourage the plant to grow up and not out. Remember, while moving your pumpkin, be extremely careful not to break or damage the vine. This is the problem with merely rotating the pumpkin to avoid that flat or odd-shaped appearance.

SAM GENDUSA
"King of the Punkin' Carvers"

SAM GENDUSA is an Oregon sculptor. He also designs and builds playground sculpture and has written and illustrated three books and numerous magazine and newspaper articles on building and sculpture. He has taught sculpture at the college, high school and elementary levels of education, including the carving of jack-o'-lanterns. His work has been featured on the CBS-TV and PBS-TV national news networks, as well as PM Magazine and numerous local television programs for the past ten years. He lives and works in Dayton, Oregon.

PHOTO CREDITS

Oregonian, October 27, 1981, Tom Treick, Photographer, *p. 43*

News-Register, McMinnville, Oregon, Friday, October 29, 1976, staff photograph, *p. 43*

Harold Westland, *p. 44*

Glenn Hashitani, *p. 66*(portrait).

Tom Ballard, *News-Register*, McMinnville, Oregon, *p. 63*

All other photographs and drawings are the author's.

Quote from St. Bernard of Clairvaux, "Apologia ad Guilb. Sancti Theodorici *abbat.*," ch. xi. *Patrol* clxxxii col. 916.

BIBLIOGRAPHY

Cavendish, Richard. *Prehistoric England*. British Heritage Press through Crown Publishers, New York, 1983.

Chippindale, Christopher. *Stonehenge Complete*. Cornell University Press, New York, 1983.

Cuyler, Margery. *The All-Around Pumpkin Book*. Holt, Reinhart & Winston, New York, 1980.

Gardener, Helen. *Art Through the Ages*. 5th Edition. Harcourt, Brace & World, New York, 1970.

Haldane, Susanne. *Faces on Places: About Gargoyles and Other Stone Creatures*. Viking Press, New York, 1980.

Kessel, Joyce K. *Halloween*. Carol/Rhoda Books, Minneapolis, MN, 1980.

Lorenz, Konrad. *On Aggression*. Harcourt, Brace & World, New York, 1963.

McCraken, Harold. *George Catlin and the Old Frontier*. Bonanza Books, 1959.

Nelson, Richard K. *Make Prayers to the Raven: A Koyukon View of the Northern Forest*. University of Chicago Press, Chicago & London, 1983.

Paterson, Lillie. *Halloween*. Garrard Publishing Co., Champaign, IL, 1963.

Sheridan, Ronald, and Ann Ross. *Gargoyles & Grotesques: Paganism in the Medieval Church*. New York Graphic Society, Boston, 1975.

Stern, Phillip Van Doren. *Prehistoric Europe: From the Stone Age to Early Greeks*. Norton & Co., New York, 1969.

Waechter, John. *Man Before History: The Making of the Past*. Elsevier/Phaidon, London & New York, 1976.

World Book Encyclopedia. Field Enterprises, Inc., 1978, Chicago.

OTHER BOOKS BY SAM GENDUSA:

If you or your friends would like a copy of *CARVING JACK-O'-LANTERNS*, please use the convenient order form below. Remember, with orders for two or more copies of this book, or any other of Mr. Gendusa's books, postage and handling will be paid.

S/G PRODUCTIONS, Box 432, Dayton, OR 97114

Please send me: ______ copy(ies) of *CARVING JACK-O'-LANTERNS* at $6.95.

Please add $1.50 postage and handling (postage paid on orders of 2 or more)

Please print Total amount enclosed $ ______

Name ______

Address ______

City ______ State ______ Zip ______